LET'S LEARN ABOUT...
THE LAND

BIG BOOK

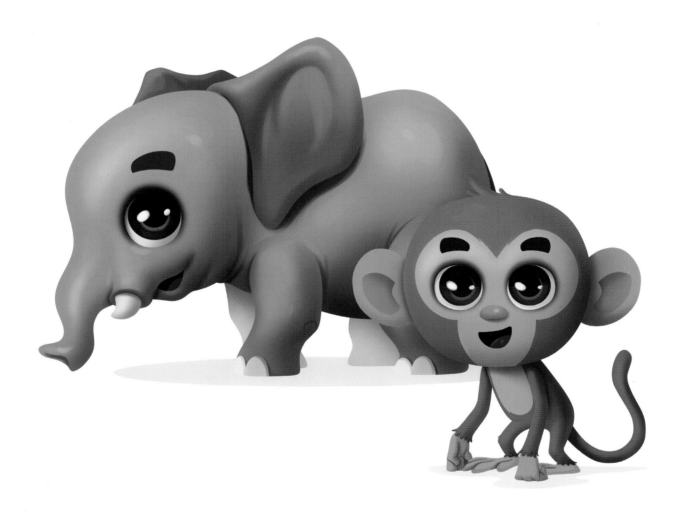

K2

TRIXIA VALLE

Pearson Education Limited
KAO Two, KAO Park, Harlow, Essex, CM17 9NA, England
and Associated Companies around the world.

First published 2020

ISBN: 978-1-292-33419-6

Set in Mundo Sans
Printed in China (SWTC/01)

Acknowledgements
The publishers and author(s) would like to thank the following people and
institutions for their feedback and comments during the development of the
material: Gisele Aga, Marcos Mendonça, Leandra Dias, Viviane Kirmeliene,
Rhiannon Ball, Simara H. Dal'Alba, Mônica Bicalho and GB Editorial.
The publishers would also like to thank all the teachers who contributed to the
development of *Let's learn about...*: Adriano de Paula Souza, Aline Ramos Teixeira
Santo, Aline Vitor Rodrigues Pina Pereira, Ana Paula Gomez Montero, Anna
Flávia Feitosa Passos, Camila Jarola, Celiane Junker Silva, Edegar França Junior,
Fabiana Reis Yoshio, Fernanda de Souza Thomaz, Luana da Silva, Michael Iacovino
Luidvinavicius, Munique Dias de Melo, Priscila Rossatti Duval Ferreira Neves,
Sandra Ferito, and schools that took part in Construindo Juntos.

Author Acknowledgements
Trixia Valle

Image Credit(s):
Pearson Education Ltd: Grupo Pictograma 20, 21, 22, 23, Marcela Gómez 8, 9,
10, 17, 18, 19, Mónica Cahué 14, 15, 16, Sheila Cabeza de Vaca 11, 12, 13, Víctor
Sandoval 27, 28, 29, 30, Visión Creativa 24, 25, 26, Ximena García Trigos 4, 5, 6, 7
Shutterstock.com: Aaltair 24, AnikaNes 24, 26, Baronb 25, Bmszealand 24, Bohbeh
25, 25, Canon Boy 24, Davizro Photography 26, Egorov Artem 26, Elnur 24, Eric
Isselee 24, Ewa Studio 24, Irina Mos 25, Lamyai 24, MalII Themd 26, MaxyM 24,
Nattan J 26, RK008 24, S_Photo 26, Sergej Onyshko 25, Sergey Novikov 24, 25, 25,
26, Shannon Jordan 25, Smereka 25, Solis Images 24, 25, 26, Wang LiQiang 24

Illustration Acknowledgements
Illustrated by Filipe Laurentino and MRS Editorial

Cover illustration © Filipe Laurentino

CONTENTS

TAKING A SHOWER

IT'S TIME FOR A SHOWER! THE SHOWER IS WARM AND NICE.

LUISA TAKES THE BOTTLE OF SOAP.

SHE USES A LOT AND DROPS IT.

THERE'S FOAM ON THE FLOOR.

THERE'S FOAM ON HER FACE AND EARS. THERE'S FOAM ON HER ARMS, HER LEGS, HER BODY, HER TOES... THERE'S EVEN FOAM ON HER MOUTH.

SHE WIGGLES HER TOES. SHE BLOWS BIG ROUND BUBBLES.

HER MOM SAYS AT THE BATHROOM DOOR, "LUISA, DON'T USE A LOT OF SOAP. ONLY A LITTLE SOAP, PLEASE!"

MOM OPENS THE BATHROOM DOOR. SHE SHAKES HER HEAD AND SAYS, "ONLY A LITTLE SOAP!"

"OOPS," LUISA SAYS. "I FORGOT!"

MOM SMILES. SHE HELPS LUISA RINSE HER FACE AND EARS. SHE HELPS HER RINSE HER ARMS, HER LEGS, HER BODY, HER TOES.

NO MORE BUBBLES. NO MORE SOAP.

LUISA IS CLEAN AND READY.

MOM KISSES HER GOOD NIGHT.

"SLEEP WELL, MY LOVE."

LUISA GOES TO BED WITH A BIG SMILE ON HER FACE.

2 THE MYSTERY OF THE MISSING PENS 🎧 03

TONY AND MIKE ARE IN THE SAME CLASSROOM.

THEY HAVE THE SAME BACKPACK. THEY HAVE THE SAME CRAYONS. THEY HAVE THE SAME BLUE PENS!

MISS SANDERS SAYS, "DEAR STUDENTS, PLEASE TAKE OUT YOUR NOTEBOOKS. TAKE OUT YOUR SCISSORS, CRAYONS, AND PEN, TOO."

TONY AND MIKE PUT THEIR THINGS ON THE TABLE AND WORK TOGETHER.

THE BELL RINGS. TIME FOR LUNCH! ALL THE STUDENTS GO TO THE PLAYGROUND.

TONY AND MIKE ARE BACK IN THE CLASSROOM. THEY CAN'T FIND THEIR BLUE PENS!

"WHERE IS MY BLUE PEN?" ASKS TONY.

"WHERE IS MY BLUE PEN?" ASKS MIKE.

MISS SANDERS SAYS, "HMM… THIS IS A MYSTERY."

THEY LOOK FOR THE PENS. MISS SANDERS FINDS TWO BLUE PENS UNDER THE TABLE.

SHE SAYS, "WHICH ONE IS YOUR PEN, TONY? WHICH ONE IS YOUR PEN, MIKE?"

"THEY ARE BOTH THE SAME!" TONY AND MIKE SAY.

MISS SANDERS SAYS, "WHAT CAN YOU DO ABOUT THIS?"

"LET'S LABEL OUR PENS!" TONY SAYS. "NO MORE MISSING PENS!" MIKE SAYS.

THEY ALL LAUGH. MIKE AND TONY TAKE THEIR PENS.

BIANCA'S MOM IS A GREAT COOK. THEY ALWAYS COOK TOGETHER.

TODAY, BIANCA AND HER COUSINS ARE IN THE MAGIC KITCHEN. THE CHILDREN ARE SURPRISED.

"OH, LOOK! THE STOVE IS BLUE," SAYS COUSIN EDDIE.

"AW! THE FRIDGE IS ORANGE," SAYS COUSIN MARY.

"OH! THE FLOOR IS GREEN! AW! THE TABLE IS PURPLE!

AND THE CUPBOARD HAS DIFFERENT COLORS, TOO!" SAYS BIANCA.

COLORS HELP MAKE MAGIC FOOD.

"LET'S BAKE A STRAWBERRY PIE!" SAYS MOM.

BIANCA OPENS THE FRIDGE.
SHE TAKES OUT THE STRAWBERRIES.

EDDIE TAKES OUT THE BUTTER AND THE EGGS.

MARY TAKES THE FLOUR AND THE SUGAR FROM
THE CUPBOARD.

THEY COOK TOGETHER. THEY HAVE FUN.
EVERYBODY SMILES.

WE HAVE FINISHED!" SAYS MOM.

"IT'S CLEANUP TIME," SAYS BIANCA.

EDDIE CLEANS THE TABLE. MARY SWEEPS THE FLOOR. BIANCA WASHES THE DISHES. EVERYBODY HELPS.

FINALLY, MOM TAKES THE PIE OUT OF THE OVEN.

YUM! EVERYBODY GETS A BIG PIECE!

4 RAIN IN THE PARK

TODAY IS SUNDAY. IT IS A BEAUTIFUL DAY!

IT IS SUNNY AND THE SKY IS BRIGHT.

WE ALL GO TO THE PARK. WE TAKE PEPPER, OUR DOG.

WE RUN AND PLAY WITH PEPPER.

WE ARE HOT AND VERY HAPPY.

LOOK! THE WIND IS BLOWING AND THE SKY IS CLOUDY AND BLACK.

IT IS RAINING! WE ALL PUT OUR RAINCOATS ON.

LOOK AT PEPPER! SHE IS COLD! SHE LOOKS SAD. POOR PEPPER!

"HMM... DO WE HAVE A JACKET?" ASKS DAD.

NOW PEPPER HAS A JACKET ON AND SHE IS NOT COLD.
PEPPER IS WARM, LIKE US. SHE IS HAPPY. SHE BARKS.
BUT SHE LOOKS VERY FUNNY WITH THE BIG JACKET ON!
WE ALL LAUGH!
RAIN OR NOT, WE ARE VERY HAPPY.

IT'S VERY EARLY IN THE MORNING.
SANDY AND JOE ARE IN THE GARDEN.
THERE ARE MANY PLANTS AND TREES.
THEY HAVE A FLASHLIGHT WITH THEM.
THEY WANT TO EXPLORE THE GARDEN.

"LOOK!" SANDY SAYS.

"WHAT IS IT?" SAYS JOE?

"THERE'S A LADYBUG ON THE FLOWER! SHE IS RED WITH BLACK SPOTS!"

"SHE IS MRS. LADYBUG," SMILES JOE.

SUDDENLY, ANOTHER LADYBUG IS ON THE FLOWER.

THEN ANOTHER, AND ANOTHER, AND ANOTHER!

"A FAMILY OF LADYBUGS ON THE FLOWERS!" LAUGHS JOE.

SUDDENLY, THERE IS A CATERPILLAR ON THE FLOWERS.

ALL THE LADYBUGS FLY AWAY.

SANDY FEELS SAD. SHE LIKES THE LADYBUGS.

JOE SAYS, "DON'T BE SAD."

"THERE ARE MANY MORE THINGS TO SEE IN THE GARDEN."

6 ICE CREAM FOR BREAKFAST 07

GRANDPA TOM IS VERY OLD.

HE HAS A BIG NOSE AND WEARS ROUND GLASSES.

HE HAS A VERY LONG GRAY BEARD.

GRANDPA TOM HAS A VEGETABLE GARDEN.

HE GROWS TOMATOES, CARROTS, LETTUCE, AND HAS A BEAUTIFUL ORANGE TREE.

GRANDPA VISITS THE TRIPLETS.

HE LOVES ICE CREAM FOR BREAKFAST.

HE WANTS ICE CREAM.

"NO," SAYS ONE TRIPLET.

"NO," SAYS ANOTHER TRIPLET.

"NO," SAYS ANOTHER TRIPLET.

"YOU CAN'T EAT ICE CREAM FOR BREAKFAST!"

"EAT AN APPLE, GRANDPA," SAYS ONE TRIPLET.

"EAT A BANANA, GRANDPA," SAYS ANOTHER TRIPLET.

"DRINK MILK, GRANDPA," SAYS ANOTHER TRIPLET.

GRANDPA TOM IS NOT HAPPY.

HE WANTS ICE CREAM FOR BREAKFAST!

THE TRIPLETS' DAD HAS AN IDEA.

THERE ARE CHOPPED BANANAS AND APPLES ON THE TABLE.

THERE IS A KNIFE ON THE TABLE.

DAD HAS A SPOON AND A BOWL.

HE MIXES THE FRUIT IN THE BOWL AND PUTS IT ON PLATES WITH A SPOON.

THEN HE PUTS ICE CREAM ON TOP OF THE FRUIT.

THE TRIPLETS ARE HAPPY. GRANDPA TOM IS HAPPY.

EVERYBODY LOVES ICE CREAM FOR BREAKFAST!

"BUT IT IS A SPECIAL TREAT. WE CAN'T EAT ICE CREAM FOR BREAKFAST EVERY DAY, OK?" SAYS DAD.

7 THE PURPLE FARM 🎧 08

MARIANA AND HER SISTER ARE AT THE PURPLE FARM.

THEY ARE WITH THEIR COUSINS MARY AND SUSAN.

MARY AND SUSAN LIVE ON THE FARM WITH UNCLE JACK.

THERE ARE MANY ANIMALS ON THE FARM.

THERE ARE MANY FRUIT TREES, TOO.

THE GIRLS SEE DUCKS.

THEY HEAR THEM QUACK.

THE GIRLS SEE SHEEP.

THEY HEAR THEM BAA.

THE GIRLS SEE HORSES.

THEY HEAR THEM NEIGH.

THE GIRLS SEE CHICKENS AND THEY SEE COWS, TOO.

THE GIRLS PLAY AND PLAY AND PLAY AT THE FARM.

IT IS VERY HOT AND THEY ARE ALL THIRSTY.

THEY FIND ORANGES UNDER THE TREES.

THEY ENJOY THE FRUIT AND THE JUICE.

IT IS SUCH A FUN DAY AT THE PURPLE FARM!

THE VET IS A HERO 🎧09

I LIKE THE NEW PARK.

IT'S MY FAVORITE PLACE.

THERE IS A FOUNTAIN AND A BENCH.
AND I CAN PLAY WITH MY FRIENDS.

AFTER THE PARK, I WALK HOME WITH MOM.

"LOOK, MOM! A HAMSTER!"

"WHERE IS IT?" MOM ASKS.

"BEHIND THE PLANTS. LOOK, MOM. IT'S HURT!"

MOM TAKES THE LITTLE HAMSTER.

"LET'S GO TO THE VET," SHE SAYS.

MOM AND I TAKE THE HAMSTER TO THE VET.

SHE TAKES THE HAMSTER WITH GENTLE HANDS.

SHE CLEANS THE HAMSTER.

SHE GIVES IT SOME MEDICINE WITH A LITTLE SPOON.

THE VET COMES BACK WITH THE HAMSTER.
"YOUR LITTLE FRIEND IS READY TO PLAY," SHE SAYS.
MOM CLAPS AND I SMILE.
THE VET IS MY HERO!

Reading Strategies

Bring as many books as you want to the classroom. Prepare a corner for reading.
You can have students bring their favorite pillow and allow them to lie down while they "read" or explore a book.

- Before showing the corresponding text to students, present a situation similar to that in the book so students begin thinking about it and relate it to their own experiences and knowledge.
- Have students work in pairs or small groups and then share their ideas with their classmates. They can also imagine a scene and draw it.
- Show the title, subtitle (if there is one), and illustrations on the title page, and ask students to predict what the story is about. Allow them to speculate and accept all ideas.
- You can show students the text and illustrations and ask if they know anything about the topic.
- Ask one or two questions related to the story, so students listen for the answers or can infer them.
- Once students have become familiarized with the story, ask them to summarize it briefly.
- Put the scenes on construction paper or cardboard, and cut out the pictures of each scene so students can put the story in order. Have students work in pairs for this activity.

Unit 1

Taking a shower

Activities with students

1. Ask students if they like to take a shower. Have them say if they like warm or cold water.
2. Have students wash their hands. Allow them to use a little soap, but remind them not to use too much soap.
3. Have students describe the texture of the soap.
4. Ask them why we can't waste water or soap.

Unit 2

The mystery of the missing pens

Activities with students

1. Ask students what their school materials are.
2. Have them work in groups of four and say how they feel when they lose something.
3. Encourage them to say how they take care of their things.
4. Elicit how important it is to respect others' belongings.
5. Encourage them to label their school materials and take care of them.

Unit 3

The magic kitchen

Activities with students

1. Ask students who cooks in their house.
2. Have them work in groups of three. Ask them how they can help in the kitchen.
3. Encourage them to think if it is better to work together or individually. Ask why.
4. Ask students to think how they feel after they have helped at home.

Unit 4

Rain in the park

Activities with students

1. Ask students to talk about their pets and where they take them. Have them say if their pets feel happy or not, and how they can tell. If they don't have a pet, tell them to think of a friend's or relative's pet.

2. In groups of three, have students reflect if pets feel hot or cold. Ask them how they can notice.

3. Ask them to think how we can protect our pets from hot and cold weather.

Unit 5

A different family

Activities with students

1. Have students reflect on their families. Encourage them to talk about the members of their family.

2. In groups of three or four, have them reflect on the differences in their families: how many brothers, sisters, grandparents, who they live with, and how each of them helps at home.

3. Reflect with students that although families are different, they are loving people and we have to accept all differences.

Unit 6

Ice cream for breakfast

Activities with students

1. In groups of three or four students, ask students what they usually have for breakfast.

2. Encourage them to say whether they like their breakfast or not and why.

3. Ask students what their favorite breakfast is and how they feel about it.

4. Tell students to notice the similarities and differences in their likes and dislikes. Reflect with students that they have to be respectful about others' opinions.

5. Ask students what kind of food they can have as a special treat.

Unit 7

The purple farm

Activities with students

1. In groups of three or four, ask students to say what a farm is. If you have pictures or other books, share them with your students.

2. Have them say what animals live on farms.

3. Reflect with students about the products we can obtain from animals (eggs, milk, wool).

4. Finally, talk about fruits we can find on a farm and ask them what their favorite fruit is.

Unit 8

The vet is a hero

Activities with students

1. In groups of three or four, have students say what their favorite place in the neighborhood is.

2. Ask them if they know any of their community workers, who they are, and what they do.

3. Reflect with students that the community workers help the people in a town and keep them safe.

4. Talk about the importance of being grateful to these people.